YOUR DISPOSITION JUST GOT BETTER:

Key steps to building good disposition

By

Beathy Splend

COPYRIGHT

TABLE OF CONTENTS

INTRODUCTION

WHAT IS DISPOSITION?

Disposition is the manner in which an individual thinks or feels about a particular individual, spot, activity or experience. Like an individual viewpoint, disposition envelops an individual's specific feelings and the manner by which they act toward a person or thing. Disposition is a particular attitude that consolidates factors like convictions, conclusions, states of mind and feelings. In some cases, disposition is alluded to as a viewpoint or mental expression that influences the manner in which individuals see their general surroundings and the manner in which they experience life, work, connections and that's only the tip of the iceberg.

Our way of behaving isn't just an element of our character, values, and inclinations, yet additionally of the circumstance. We decipher our current circumstance, figure out reactions, and act as needs be.

Keeping an uplifting outlook all through your own and proficient life can assist you with tracking down solid survival techniques for stressors and difficulties. With an uplifting outlook, you might have the option to conquer hindrances all the more effectively, track down additional chances to offer thanks in your day to day existence and even manufacture significant ways toward accomplishing your fantasies. While encouraging an uplifting perspective on an everyday premise can sometimes feel testing, particularly when you experience pressure in your life, it's a beneficial undertaking to embrace. In this article, we will examine what disposition is, components of good disposition and ways to keep an uplifting outlook.

CHAPTER 1

DISCERNMENT

Discernment might be characterized as the interaction with which people distinguish and decipher natural boosts. Makes human discernment so fascinating that we don't exclusively answer the improvements in our current circumstance. We go past the data that is available in our current circumstance, give specific consideration to certain parts of the climate, and disregard different components that might be promptly evident to others. Our view of the climate isn't altogether sane. For instance, have you at any point seen that while looking at a paper or a news Site, data that is fascinating or critical to you leaps out of the page and grabs your attention? On the off chance that you are an avid supporter, while looking down the pages you may promptly see a news article portraying the most recent progress of your group. On the off chance that you are the parent of a finicky eater, a counsel section on baby taking care of might be the main thing you see while checking the page out. So what we find in the climate is an element of what we esteem, our requirements, our feelings of trepidation, and our feelings. Infact, what we find in the climate might be unbiased, absolute off-base in view of our character, values, or feelings. For instance, one examination showed that when individuals who feared bugs were shown insects, they erroneously felt that the bug was advancing toward them. In this segment, we will depict a few normal propensities we take part in while seeing items or others, hand the results of such discernments. Our inclusion of predispositions and propensities in discernment isn't comprehensive — there are numerous different predispositions and propensities on our social insight.

Visual Discernment

Our visual discernment certainly goes past the actual data accessible to us. We, first of all, extrapolate from the data accessible to us. Our visual discernment is frequently one-sided on the grounds that we don't see objects in detachment. The differentiation between our focal point of consideration and the rest of the climate might cause an item to seem greater or more modest. The differentiation between the central article and the articles encompassing it might make an item greater or more modest to our eye.

How do these propensities impact conduct in associations? You might have understood that the way that our visual discernment is defective may make observer declarations broken and one-sided. How do we have at least some idea whether the representative you judge to be dedicated, quick, and flawless is truly similar to that? Is it truly obvious, or would we say we are contrasting this individual with others in the prompt climate? Or on the other hand suppose that you could do without one of your companions and you feel that this individual is continually riding the Internet during work hours. Is it true or not that you are certain? Have you truly seen this individual surf irrelevant Sites, or is it conceivable that the individual was riding the Internet for business related purposes? Our one-sided visual insight might prompt some unacceptable derivations about individuals around us.

Self-Discernment

People are inclined to make mistakes and inclinations while seeing themselves. Also, the sort of inclination individuals have relies upon their character. Many individuals experience the ill of self-upgrade predisposition. This is the propensity to misjudge our exhibition and capacities and see ourselves in a more sure light than others see us. Individuals who have a self-absorbed character are especially dependent upon this predisposition, however numerous others are as yet inclined to misjudging their capacities. Simultaneously, others have the restricting limit, which might be named as self-destruction inclination. This is the propensity for individuals to misjudge their presentation, underestimate capacities, and witness occasions such that places them in a more bad light. We might expect that individuals with low confidence might be especially inclined to make this mistake. These propensities have genuine ramifications for conduct in associations. For instance, individuals who experience the ill effects of outrageous degrees of self-upgrade propensities may not comprehend the reason why they are not getting advanced or compensated, while the people who tend to self-destroy may project low certainty and assume more fault for their disappointments than needed.

While seeing themselves, people are likewise dependent upon the bogus agreement blunder. Basically, we misjudge that we are so like others. We expect that anything that peculiarities we have are shared by a bigger number of individuals than as a general rule. Individuals who bring office supplies back home, lie to their chief or partners, or assume praise for others' work to excel may truly feel that these ways of behaving are more normal than they truly are. The issue for conduct in associations is that, when individuals accept that a way of behaving is normal and ordinary, they might rehash the conduct all the more uninhibitedly. Under certain conditions this might prompt an elevated degree of untrustworthy or even unlawful ways of behaving.

Social Discernment

How we see others in our current circumstance is additionally formed by our qualities, feelings, sentiments, and character. In addition, how we see others will impact our way of behaving, which thus will mold the way of behaving of the individual we are associating with.

One of the variables biasing our insight is generalizations. Generalizations will be speculations in light of gathering qualities. For instance, accepting that ladies are more helpful than men, or men are more confident than ladies, is a generalization. Generalizations might be positive, negative, or impartial. Individuals have a characteristic inclination to order the data around them to figure out their current circumstance. What makes generalizations possibly oppressive and a perceptual inclination is the propensity to sum up from a gathering to a specific person. Assuming the conviction that men are more confident than ladies prompts picking a man over a similarly (or possibly more) qualified female possibility for a position, the choice will be one-sided, possibly unlawful, and unreasonable. Generalizations frequently cause what is going on called an unavoidable outcome. This cycle happens when individuals naturally act as though a laid out generalization is precise, which prompts a receptive way of behaving from the other party that affirms the generalization. In the event that you have a generalization, for example, "Asians are well disposed," you are bound to be cordial toward an Asian yourself. Since you are treating the other individual better, the reaction you get may likewise be better, affirming your unique conviction that Asians are well disposed. Obviously, the exact inverse is likewise evident. Assume you trust that "youthful representatives are good-for-nothings." You are less inclined to give a youthful worker elevated degrees of obligation or fascinating and testing tasks.

The outcome might be that the youthful representative answering to you might turn out to be progressively exhausted working and begin fooling around, validating your premonitions that youngsters are loafers! Generalizations persevere in light of a cycle called specific discernment. Specific discernment essentially implies that we give particular consideration to parts of the climate while overlooking different parts. At the point when we notice our current circumstance, we see what we need to see and overlook data that might appear to be awkward. Here is a fascinating illustration of how specific discernment drives our insight to be formed by the unique circumstance: As a component of a social trial, in 2007 the Washington Post paper organized Joshua Ringer, the universally acclaimed violin virtuoso, to act in an edge of the Metro station in Washington DC. The violin he was playing was valued at $3.5 million, and tickets for Chime's shows typically cost around $100. During the busy time in which he played for 45 minutes, just a single individual remembered him, a couple understood that they were hearing exceptional music, and he made just $32 in tips. When you see somebody playing at the metro station, could you anticipate that they should be phenomenal?

Our experiences, assumptions, and convictions will shape which occasions we notice and which occasions we disregard. For instance, the useful foundation of chiefs influences the progressions they see in their current circumstance. Chiefs with a foundation in deals and promoting see the progressions in the interest for their item, while leaders with a foundation in data innovation may all the more promptly see the progressions in the innovation the organization is utilizing. Particular insight might propagate generalizations, since we are less inclined to see occasions that conflict with our convictions. An individual who accepts that men drive better compared to ladies might be bound to see ladies driving ineffectively than men driving inadequately. Thus, a generalization is kept up with in light of the fact that data running against the norm may not arrive at our mind.

Suppose we saw data that conflicts with our convictions. What then? Tragically, this is no assurance that we will alter our convictions and biases. In the first place, when we see models that conflict with our generalizations, we will quite often think of subcategories. For instance, when individuals who accept that ladies are more helpful see a female who is decisive, they might group this individual as a "lifelong lady." Hence, the guide running against the norm doesn't disregard the generalization, and on second thought is cleared up as an exemption for the standard. Second, we may essentially limit the data. In one review, individuals who were either for or against capital punishment were shown two examinations, one appearance benefits from capital punishment and the other limiting any advantages. Individuals dismissed the review that conflicted with their conviction as systemically substandard and really built up the faith in their unique position much more. As such, attempting to expose individuals' convictions or recently settled conclusions with information may not be guaranteed to help.

Another perceptual inclination that might influence work conduct is that of initial feelings. The initial feelings we structure about individuals will generally have an enduring effect. As a matter of fact, initial feelings, once shaped, are shockingly versatile to opposite data. Regardless of whether individuals are informed that the initial feelings were brought about by off base data, individuals clutch them somewhat. That's what the explanation is, when we structure initial feelings, they become free of the proof that made them. Any data we get going against the norm doesn't effectively alter the first impression. Envision the primary day you met your associate Rossy. She treated you in a discourteous way and when you requested her assistance, she dismissed you. You might shape the conviction that she is a discourteous and pointless individual. Afterward, you might hear that her mom is extremely debilitated and she is exceptionally worried. As a general rule she might have been curiously worried on the day you met her. Assuming you had met her on an alternate day, you might have believed that she is a truly decent individual who is surprisingly focused nowadays. Yet, odds are your feeling that she is inconsiderate and pointless won't change in any event, when you catch wind of her mom. All things being equal, this new snippet of data will be added to the first: She is impolite, pointless, and her mom is wiped out. Monitoring this propensity and intentionally opening your psyche to new data might safeguard you against a portion of the drawbacks of this inclination. Additionally, it would be for your potential benefit to give cautious consideration to the initial feelings you make, especially during prospective employee meetings.

CHAPTER 2

CERTAINTY

Certainty is a healthy identity confirmation emerging from one's enthusiasm for one's own capacities or characteristics. It is the confidence in oneself and one's capacity to prevail in a specific circumstance or to achieve a particular errand. Certainty can be worked through experience, mindfulness, and a positive outlook. A significant characteristic can emphatically influence different parts of life, including individual connections, vocation achievement, and generally prosperity. Sure individuals frequently show specific ways of behaving that mirror their confidence.

A few normal ways of behaving of sure people include:

Keeping in touch: Certain individuals will quite often keep in touch during discussions, showing their commitment and self-assuredness.

Speaking Plainly and Emphatically: They talk with lucidity and self-assuredness, offering their viewpoints and assessments with certainty.

Undivided attention: Certain people are many times great audience members, showing real interest in others and participating in significant discussions.

Stepping up: They are proactive and ready to start to lead the pack in different circumstances, showing trust in their capacities.

Receptiveness to Criticism: Certain individuals are available to valuable input and view it as a chance for development as opposed to a danger to their confidence.

Non-verbal communication: Their non-verbal communication frequently radiates certainty, with open and loosened up stances, expressive signals, and a solid, grounded presence.

Defining Limits: Sure people are happy with defining limits and saying no while essential, focusing on their prosperity and values.

Versatility: They are versatile and strong even with difficulties, showing trust in their capacity to explore change and defeat obstructions.

These ways of behaving by and large add to a sure and confident disposition that can decidedly influence individual and expert connections.

Check these interesting models out:

- You remain solitary in a get-together without being excessively reluctant or awkward.

- You come to school/work environments with a shaved head and mean remarks of your companions don't irritate you much.

You approach the stage and talk your heart out, regardless of individuals' thought process/feel about you as a "speaker".

- You eat alone in a food joint without looking at others' faces.

- You practice at home, notwithstanding realizing that you are an "ectomorph" or "hard gainer".

- You say "NO" to individuals without being quelled by their horrendous decisions.
- You dare to approach a total outsider and make fascinating discussions.
- You don't look for endorsement from others.
- You grin just when you truly would not joke about this.

Reasons for low certainty

Careless guardians: Having guardians that weren't there when you really wanted help.

Objecting guardians: Never getting positive input as a kid can leave you pursuing endorsement from others.

Actual uncertainties: Not having the option to satisfy society's norms of what's 'great'.

Past experience: An individual who was manhandled could accept they merited it and that is unfavorable to their self-esteem.

Nervousness and misery: These issues can prevent most aspects of your life, and fearlessness is one of them.

Awful companions: Having companions who are phony and manipulative.

Negative self-talk: Eventually, they fostered this example and presently it runs them.

Contrasting themselves: Individuals will more often than not contrast their section 8 and somebody's part 30. It's unreasonable.

Fix to low certainty

Before you gain certainty, you want confidence. To put stock in yourself and lift your certainty, know yourself first.

You want to fabricate your confidence to dispose of that sensation of not being sufficient. Building confidence is quite possibly the best choice throughout everyday life. It's a major need. You really want to feel you are authentic in yourself. You should have the option to track down assets in yourself. You want to feel significantly better acting naturally. How?

To begin with, realize what your identity is. Second, acknowledge what your identity is. Third, be what your identity is. Fourth, Be happy with being what your identity is. Fifth, love what your identity is. Foster your character. Show your character. Be thoughtful, yet decisive.

Foster these standards, you will feel sure around others:

Individual Character: Know what your identity is. Know about your reality. Realize you are unique, special, however equivalent to every other person. Be associated with your inward you. Act naturally. Try not to attempt to resemble others. You want mindfulness. You exist so you are an individual. You can't find anything that will demonstrate that you're not human. Be straightforward with yourself. You are so you exist and you should exist.

Self-acknowledgment: Acknowledge to be as are you. Since you are as you are, you have the right to live that way. Quit contrasting yourself and others. Be thankful for what your identity is.

Great Confidence: Know your value. Quit accusing yourself or others. See your significance. Be a jewel for yourself. Confidence. Love yourself since it's an obligation. You are exceptional, remember it. You merit regard, regardless of what your identity is. The principal individual who needs to have a high regard for you it's you. How could any other individual have a high regard of you in the event that you have a low regard of yourself? Be sensible. You need to deal with yourself. Characterize what your identity is. Like it and love it. Be a companion for yourself. Address yourself like you will accomplish for a companion. Quit naming yourself with nonsensical marks like you are useless, individuals are a higher priority than you or everyone is superior to you or you feel sub-par compared to everyone. You, most importantly, don't actually know others and quit thinking often about others' disposition, capacity or abilities. That is nothing you should be worrying about. Your business is yourself. Know what your identity is, love it then share it with individuals. Not every person will like you. It's life. Yet, what difference does it make? There could be no more excellent love than confidence. God love is above it obviously. You really want genuine love. Love yourself for everything in you: your characteristics, your blemishes, your encounters and everything. You are commendable. You matter. You need to acknowledge reality regardless of what occurs in your life that makes you think others are superior to you. Your impression of low confidence isn't the truth. Actually you are commendable and equivalent to each person.

Self-assurance: See yourself as skilled. Trust in yourself. Trust yourself. Begin allowing yourself an opportunity. Begin to have confidence in yourself. Propel yourself. You need to battle with the trepidation you have inside and the little voice that represses you. Be more grounded than your trepidation.

Decisiveness: Put yourself out there, your sentiments, your necessities. Be the genuine you. Do what you truly believe you should do except if it's not unlawful. Say no when you think no. Try not to allow individuals to choose your life. Represent yourself. No one is superior to you to make it happen, except for God himself.

Be positive: Simply take just the positive piece of any circumstance. Being positive is the main answer for progress. No one has known about a gloomy individual who has achievement. It's sort of incomprehensible.

Dare: Take your obligations. You need to confront your apprehensions. Recollecting that mental fortitude isn't the nonappearance of dread however confronting what is happening with dread. You need to make the initial steps. Try not to trust that individuals will think often about you. On the off chance that you can work on something for yourself, get it done. Try not to be detached. Be dynamic. Assume command over your life. Assuming you like somebody or love somebody, show it to that individual. Try not to trust that the other individual will make the initial step. You can hang tight for what seems like forever. Face challenges. Be quick to start things. Try not to hang tight for other people. You have the right like any other individual to take drives. Be innovative.

Be OK with being powerless: Acknowledge to be a human being. Feel alright with dismissal. Try not to think about it literally. Acknowledge your feelings, your sentiments. Be OK with your freedoms. You reserve the option to adore individuals or to be cherished. You can partake in your life too.

Acknowledge your imperfections. Acknowledge to be flawed. Try not to act over the top with yourself.

Quit thinking or thinking often about others' thought process: Quit looking for individuals' endorsement or love. Quit being thoughtful when you would rather not be caring. I realize there are social standards, yet don't make an effort not to be kind to individuals. There is no greatness in doing that.

Be loose: Express no to biases or edifices. Be cool with individuals. Attempt to consider life to be a gift. Attempt to associate with individuals as opposed to seeing individuals by classification. Make an effort not to condemn people.

Quit contrasting yourself as well as other people: Contrasting yourself and individuals is the system of mediocrity complex. Stop doing that. Rather than that, foster appreciation. Think about the beneficial things that occurred in your life. Think about existence as a gift. Quit griping, however work on yourself to be your best self.

Quit looking for individuals' endorsement: You really want to look for your self-endorsement, You really want to consider your thought process as surprisingly significant or possibly as equivalents, You should know that you needn't bother with individuals' affection to adore yourself or to be content, Quit trying to satisfy everyone. Begin carrying on with your life as the entertainer of your life. You need to know that having a sweetheart or beauty won't make you more joyful assuming that you actually have no self-esteem. Know about your value. It's not possible for anyone to cherish you in the event that you don't adore yourself first. You are an item. In the event that you don't do a great promotion for an item, no one will like it. Sell yourself well. Love yourself. Value what your identity is. Know about your assets. Find what your identity is. Protect yourself. Represent yourself. You sentence yourself to a hopeless life on the off chance that you are as yet looking for individuals' endorsement. You really want to quit doing that!!

Follow those means. Find yourself once more. Happy go lucky about yourself. Love yourself and afterward go to individuals.

I guarantee you, you will conquer that serious insecurity or low self-esteem.

CHAPTER 3

INSPIRATION

Energy is a perspective portrayed by the propensity to zero in on the positive qualities in some random circumstance, to move toward difficulties with confidence, and to keep a confident point of view. It includes developing an outlook that underscores appreciation, strength, and a helpful way to deal with critical thinking. Inspiration can add to by and large prosperity and emotional wellness, and it can likewise affect how people interface with others and explore their everyday encounters.

ADVANTAGES

Positive reasoning doesn't imply that you overlook upsetting circumstances throughout everyday life. An uplifting outlook is a way you approach life all the more emphatically. You think the best will occur, not just plain terrible. Likewise, an inspirational perspective empowers you to adapt better to disagreeable life circumstances. Subsequently, you will generally bring down the pace of pressure, misery and diminish dangers of cardiovascular infection. Furthermore, when you are hopeful, you will generally have better ways of life, for example, doing more proactive tasks and having a better eating regimen.

Joy

One of the most outstanding impacts of a positive disposition is that you will become hopelessly enamored with yourself. As people, love is something we as a whole lengthy for. At the point when you love yourself, your life and individuals around you, you will be genuinely cheerful. At the point when you have an inspirational perspective towards life, your general state of mind will be gotten to the next level. You will acquire conditions of harmony, bliss, quiet and energy from your inward world. Uplifting perspective incites grins and encourages you. Hence, you want to track down ways of rehearsing good feelings in your day to day existence to feel blissful as who could do without joy?

Fearlessness

Good faith and inspiration can assist you with supporting your self-assurance, which is one of the best impacts of a positive outlook. As you are good and you love yourself, you begin to feel more certain about the thing you are doing, and the weaknesses disappear. You won't ever question your capacities and afterward you will quite often get familiar with life. Likewise, you manage life in a vastly improved way by expanding potential outcomes and opening your brain to new encounters.

Victory

Do you have at least some idea that an uplifting perspective towards life can bring about progress? Your disposition has some control over your life. Assuming that you are constantly staying with negative reasoning in your mind, you can anticipate disappointment. Nonetheless, assuming your considerations are positive, you will frame activities that assist you with turning out to be more useful and more successful. Positive reasoning empowers you to see life gives all the more decidedly, then you will frame improved arrangements or plans to manage them. Thus, an uplifting perspective doesn't simply bring you warm sentiments yet additionally assists you with investigating your gifts and gaining accomplishments.

Association with others

On the off chance that you are a positive and hopeful individual, you are not excessively worried about your own issues. Thus, you are available to individuals and you effectively interface with others around you. Plus, when you have an uplifting perspective, you are upbeat to other people who might feel cheerful by your presence. Then, at that point, you have more opportunities to shape associations with others and to work on your organizations, which is one of the best impacts of a positive disposition .

Notwithstanding the thing you are doing throughout everyday life, consistently utilize positive reasoning consistently, you will perceive how surprisingly it helps your life in each circumstance.

Here are rules/things to snatch Inspiration

- Drilling down things of which you are thankful for.
- Endeavors to chop down virtual entertainment life.
- Listen to a cheery playlist.
- Chuckle whenever you need.
- Call someone,who makes you great.
- Yoga
- Books
- Survey on the web, web journals.
- Positive assertion reflects ordinary.
- High-five somebody
- BE certain
- Contemplate
- Inspirational digital recordings.

- Work out.

- Help somebody in a day.

- Plan an excursion every so often.

- Motivating statements.

- Taking care of oneself.

- Make and immediately take advantage of opportunities in life.

CHAPTER 4

DEVELOPMENT OUTLOOK

What's the significance here to have a development outlook? Having a development disposition implies accepting that an individual's capacities aren't natural yet can be worked on through exertion, learning and industriousness. A development outlook is about the disposition with which an individual countenances difficulties, how they process disappointments, and how they adjust and develop thus. In business, the capacity to learn and develop after a misfortune is one of the keys to progress. Individuals with a development disposition are continuously searching for ways of improving, whether that implies mastering new abilities, evaluating new procedures, or rolling out huge improvements to how they work. At the point when they experience a mishap, an individual with a development disposition can recuperate all the more rapidly and could see unforeseen issues not as obstructions to advance but rather as any open doors for development.

Cultivating this positive, groundbreaking approach can be a fundamental apparatus for anybody in business, whether they're simply beginning or are prepared business visionaries. A development outlook can be the contrast between just making due or flourishing in the present quickly changing business scene.

Qualities of a development outlook

So how can you say whether you have a development outlook? The response isn't clear all of the time. As far as one might be concerned, there's no such thing as an unadulterated development disposition . The majority of us take on various mentalities relying upon the circumstance we're in. For instance, you could face challenges and act all the more straightforwardly in business, however you value routine and be more impervious to change in your own life. No unmistakable line isolates the two sorts of reasoning, yet here are a few signs that propose you could incline in the direction of a development outlook.

- You accept that accomplishments are down to exertion, not simply inborn ability.
- You're willing to gain from your errors and track down esteem in analysis.
- You accept that your knowledge and capacity can be created.
- You're willing to seek clarification on pressing issues and concede when you don't know something.
- You search out testing errands and face gambles.

Advantages of having a development outlook.

Whether it's ready to go or daily existence, cultivating a development disposition can have both short-and long haul benefits. Here are only a couple of instances of how it can help.

A development outlook can assist you with turning out to be stronger notwithstanding mishaps. At the point when you go over a tough spot, you're bound to approach it as a test to be defeated as opposed to motivation to call it quits. You become better ready to persevere despite difficulty and accomplish your objectives.

A development outlook can assist you with turning out to be more versatile. As opposed to feeling overpowered or compromised by large changes, you're bound to consider them to be chances to learn, develop, and reexamine yourself. You can embrace new difficulties and use them for your potential benefit.

A development disposition can assist you with developing an uplifting outlook. At the point when you trust that your ability to further develop your own gifts is limitless, disappointment quotes being something to be terrified of. You can move toward difficulties with hopefulness and certainty, which makes you a superior chief and cultivates a more sure workplace.

Development disposition versus fixed attitude.

Assuming a development outlook accepts that specific qualities can be improved with exertion and preparation, a proper disposition accepts we're left with the qualities we have until the end of time. That could seem like something terrible, yet there are still a few benefits to having a decent outlook. While it's generally expected outlined as a feeling of dread toward change and development, a decent outlook esteems a moderate and hazard opposed way to deal with carrying on with work. Those with fixed outlooks are much of the time better at zeroing in on the things they know they're great at and digging that mastery for extraordinary outcomes.

The most effective method to foster a development outlook.

The mentalities we have right currently were shaped by many years of individual experience, yet that doesn't mean they can't change. Research lets us know that our cerebrums are continuously making new associations, even as we age. With preparing and self-restraint, it's feasible to move from a proper outlook to a development disposition .

Instances of development disposition thinking.

You make little strides every day toward your objectives:

Change doesn't work out more or less by accident, yet in the event that you can fabricate little, positive activities into your day to day everyday practice —, for example, pondering after you clean your teeth — you can transform them into propensities.

You escape your usual range of familiarity:
Take on an undertaking accomplishing something you have no involvement in. Attempt another side interest, play another game, or challenge yourself to accomplish something you've never finished, like talking before a group of people.

You adapt to any and all challenges:
It requires investment to foster a development outlook, so don't be daunted on the off chance that you don't get results. All things being equal, center around consistency. Make positive strides every day and trust that the outcomes will come in time.

You search out new viewpoints:

Books are a priceless wellspring of groundbreaking thoughts and perspectives, and can open you to novel approaches to seeing the world that you hadn't considered previously. Investigating new topics with a receptive outlook can likewise assist you with survey existing difficulties in another light, making it more straightforward to recognize arrangements you could somehow have missed.

CHAPTER 5

EMOTIONAL QUOTIENT

Emotional quotient (also called close to home remainder or EQ) is the capacity to grasp, use, and deal with your own feelings in good ways to ease pressure, impart successfully, understand others, conquer difficulties and stop struggle. Emotional quotient assists you with building more grounded connections, prevailing at school and work, and accomplishing your profession and individual objectives. It can likewise assist you with interfacing with your sentiments, transform the goal right into it, and arrive at informed conclusions about what makes the biggest difference to you.

For what reason is the capacity to appreciate people at their core so significant?

As far as we might be concerned, not the savviest individuals who are the best or the most satisfied throughout everyday life. You likely know individuals who are scholastically splendid but are socially awkward and fruitless at work or in their own connections. Scholarly capacity or your IQ (level of intelligence) isn't enough all alone to make progress throughout everyday life. Indeed, your level of intelligence can assist you with getting into school, yet your EQ will assist you with dealing with the pressure and feelings while confronting your last tests of the year. Intelligence level and EQ exist as a couple and are best when they work off each other.

Emotional quotient influences:

Your presentation at the everyday schedule: High ability to appreciate people on a deeper level can assist you with exploring the social intricacies of the working environment, lead and propel others, and succeed in your profession. As a matter of fact, with regards to measuring significant work competitors, many organizations presently rate Emotional quotient as significant as specialized capacity and utilize EQ testing prior to employing.

Your actual well-being: Assuming you can't deal with your feelings, you are likely not dealing with your pressure all things considered. This can prompt serious medical issues. Uncontrolled pressure raises circulatory strain, stifles the invulnerable framework, expands the gamble of coronary failures and strokes, adds to barrenness, and rates up the maturing system. The initial step to further developing the ability to appreciate people on a deeper level is to figure out how to oversee pressure.

Your psychological well-being: Uncontrolled feelings and stress can likewise influence your emotional wellness, making you helpless against uneasiness and wretchedness. On the off chance that you can't comprehend, become familiar with, or deal with your feelings, you'll likewise battle major areas of strength for shape. This thus can leave you feeling desolate and confined and further worsen any psychological well-being issues.

Your connections: By understanding your feelings and how to control them, you're better ready to communicate how you feel and comprehend how others are feeling. This permits you to impart all the more and produce more grounded connections, both at work and in your own life.

Your social knowledge: Being in line with your feelings fills a social need, associating you to others and your general surroundings. Social knowledge empowers you to perceive companionship from adversaries, measure someone else's advantage in you, diminish pressure, balance your sensory system through friendly correspondence, and feel cherished and blissful.

Building your Emotional Quotient

The abilities that make up Emotional Quotient can be learned whenever. Nonetheless, it's memorable that there is a contrast between basically finding out about EQ and applying that information to your life. Since you realize you ought to accomplish something doesn't mean you will — particularly when you become overpowered by pressure, which can abrogate your best expectations. To change conduct in manners that are exceptional under tension, you really want to figure out how to conquer pressure at the time, and in your connections, to remain genuinely mindful.

The vital abilities for building your EQ and working on your capacity to deal with feelings and associate with others are:

- Self-administration
- Mindfulness
- Social mindfulness
- Relationship the board

Key Ability 1: Self-administration

For you to draw in your EQ, you should have the option to utilize your feelings to settle on productive conclusions about your way of behaving. At the point when you become excessively focused, you can fail to keep a grip on your feelings and the capacity to act nicely and suitably.

Contemplate when stress has overpowered you. Was it simple to think plainly or pursue a reasonable choice? Most likely not. At the point when you become excessively pushed, your capacity to both think obviously and precisely survey feelings — your own and others' — becomes compromised.

Feelings are significant snippets of data that enlighten you concerning yourself as well as other people, yet even with pressure that removes us from our usual range of familiarity, we can become overwhelmed and neglect to keep a hold on ourselves. With the capacity to oversee pressure and remain sincerely present, you can figure out how to get disturbing data without allowing it to abrogate your contemplations and discretion. You'll have the option to settle on decisions that permit you to control imprudent sentiments and ways of behaving, deal with your feelings in solid ways, step up, completely finish responsibilities, and adjust to evolving conditions.

Key ability 2: Mindfulness

Overseeing pressure is only the initial step to building Emotional quotient . The study of connection demonstrates that your ongoing profound experience is probably an impression of your initial valuable experience. Your capacity to oversee center sentiments like resentment, misery, dread, and delight frequently relies upon the quality and consistency of your initial life profound encounters. On the off chance that your essential overseer as a baby got it and esteemed your feelings, it's probable your feelings have become important resources in grown-up life. Yet, in the event that your close to home encounters as a newborn child were befuddling, compromising or excruciating, it's probably you've attempted to move away from your feelings.

Yet, having the option to interface with your feelings — having a second-to-second association with your changing profound experience — is the way to understanding what feeling means for your viewpoints and activities.

Do you encounter sentiments that flow,encountering an endless series of feelings as your encounters change from one second to another?

Are your feelings joined by actual impressions that you experience in places like your stomach, throat, or chest?

Do you encounter individual sentiments and feelings, like annoyance, trouble, dread, and happiness, every one of which is obvious in unobtrusive looks?

Could you at any point encounter extraordinary sentiments that are sufficiently able to catch both your consideration and that of others?

Do you focus on your feelings? Do they factor into your independent direction? Assuming that any of these encounters are new, you might have "turned down" or "switched off" your feelings. To construct EQ — and become sincerely solid — you should reconnect to your center feelings, acknowledge them, and become OK with them. You can accomplish this through the act of care.

Care is the act of deliberately concentrating on the current second — and without judgment. The development of care has been established in Buddhism, yet most religions incorporate a comparable petition or reflection procedure of some sort or another. Care assists shift your distraction with thought toward an enthusiasm for the occasion, your physical and close to home sensations, and welcomes a bigger point of view on life. Care quiets and centers you, making you more mindful all the while.

You should figure out how to oversee pressure first, so you'll feel more open to reconnecting to solid or horrendous feelings and changing how you experience and answer your sentiments.

Key ability 3: Social mindfulness

Social mindfulness empowers you to perceive and decipher the for the most part nonverbal prompts others are continually utilizing to speak with you. These prompts let you in on how others are truly feeling, how their profound state is changing from one second to another, and what means a lot to them. At the point when gatherings convey comparable nonverbal prompts, you're ready to peruse and grasp the power elements and share close to home encounters of the gathering. So, you're sympathetic and socially agreeable. Care is a partner of profound and social mindfulness

To assemble social mindfulness, you really want to perceive the significance of care in the social cycle. All things considered, you can't get on unobtrusive nonverbal prompts when you're in your own head, contemplating different things, or essentially daydreaming on your telephone. Social mindfulness requires your presence at the time. While a significant number of us highly esteem a capacity to perform various tasks, this implies that you'll miss the unobtrusive close to home movements occurring in others that assist you with completely grasping them.

You are bound to further your social objectives by saving different contemplations and zeroing in on the actual communication.

Following the progression of someone else's personal reactions is a compromise cycle that expects you to likewise focus on the progressions in your own close to home insight.

Focusing on others doesn't decrease your own mindfulness. By managing the time and work to truly focus on others, you'll really acquire knowledge into your own profound state as well as your qualities and convictions. For instance, assuming you feel distress hearing others express specific perspectives, you'll have mastered something significant about yourself.

Key ability 4: Relationship the executives

Cooperating with other people is a cycle that starts with profound mindfulness and your capacity to perceive and comprehend what others are encountering. When profound mindfulness is in play, you can successfully foster extra friendly/close to home abilities that will make your connections more powerful, productive, and satisfying.

Become mindful of how successfully you utilize nonverbal correspondence. It's difficult to try not to send nonverbal messages to others about what you think and feel. The many muscles in the face, particularly those around the eyes, nose, mouth and temple, assist you with silently conveying your own feelings as well as perusing other people groups' personal plans. The profound piece of your mind is dependably on — and regardless of whether you overlook its messages — others will not. Perceiving the nonverbal messages that you ship off others can have an immense impact in working on your connections.

Use humor and play to ease pressure. Humor, chuckling and play are regular counteractants to push. They reduce your weights and assist you with keeping things in context. Giggling brings your sensory system into balance, lessening pressure, quieting you down, honing your brain and making you more empathic.

Figure out how to consider struggle to be a potential chance to develop nearer to other people. Struggle and conflicts are unavoidable in human connections. Two individuals couldn't realistically have similar requirements, feelings, and assumptions consistently. Nonetheless, that shouldn't need to be something terrible. Settling clashes in sound, useful ways can fortify trust between individuals. At the point when struggle isn't seen as compromising or rebuffing, it encourages opportunity, imagination, and wellbeing in connections

CHAPTER 6

FLEXIBILITY

Flexibility is the capacity to conform to new circumstances and changes. It includes being receptive, adaptable, and able to learn. Versatility isn't just about having the option to deal with transform; it is additionally about being proactive and expecting change before it works out. Workers who are versatile can undoubtedly shift gears, take on new jobs, and explore through vulnerability effortlessly.

While certain people might be normally versatile, an expertise can be mastered and created. One method for developing flexibility is to embrace change and search for amazing chances to learn and develop. This can include taking on new obligations, attempting new things, and searching out criticism. Furthermore, developing a development disposition can assist people with turning out to be more versatile. That is accepting that abilities and capacities can be created through commitment and difficult work. At last, putting resources into preparing and advancement can assist representatives with mastering new abilities and remain in front of industry changes.

Flexibility is a basic expertise that representatives need to have in the present high speed and steadily changing workplace. By understanding what versatility is, the reason it is important, and how to develop it, representatives can situate themselves for progress and flourish in any circumstance.

The Advantages of Versatility in Group Elements

Versatility assumes a critical part in the outcome of any group. It is the capacity to acclimate to changes in the climate, conditions, and assumptions. In the present quick moving world, change is unavoidable, and groups should have the option to adjust to those changes to remain important.

The advantages of versatility in group elements are various and can have the effect of progress and disappointment. From further developed correspondence to expanded efficiency, flexibility is critical to flourishing in change.

1. Further developed Correspondence: Groups that are versatile are better prepared to actually convey. At the point when changes happen, colleagues should have the option to change their correspondence styles to fit the new conditions. Groups that are not versatile may battle with this and experience breakdowns in correspondence that can adversely affect efficiency and confidence.

2. **Expanded Efficiency:** Groups that are versatile can rapidly acclimate to changes in responsibility and assumptions. This adaptability permits them to work all the more proficiently and successfully, bringing about expanded efficiency. For instance, a group that is dealing with a venture and

experiences unforeseen obstacles might have to move their methodology or timetable. Versatility permits them to make those changes rapidly and push ahead.

3. **Upgraded Imagination:** Flexibility can likewise prompt improved inventiveness and advancement. At the point when groups are available to change, they are bound to investigate groundbreaking thoughts and approaches. This can prompt leap forwards in thinking and critical thinking that might not have been imaginable in any case. For instance, a group that is dealing with another item might have to turn their methodology in view of new market patterns. Flexibility permits them to investigate groundbreaking

thoughts and techniques to deal with those patterns.

4. **Further developed Assurance:** Groups that are versatile frequently have higher resolve. At the point when colleagues feel that they are prepared to deal with transformation, they feel more positive about their capacities and are bound to remain spurred and locked in. This can prompt a more sure workplace and improved results generally speaking. Flexibility is the way to effective overall vibes. Groups that are versatile are better prepared to deal with change, convey really, and work all the more productively. By embracing versatility, groups can upgrade their imagination, increment efficiency , and further develop confidence.

Methodologies for Creating Flexibility Abilities

Flexibility is a pivotal expertise that empowers a person to conform to new circumstances, changing conditions and different conditions without any problem. It is a fundamental component for flourishing in the high speed , complex, and questionable corporate world. In a quickly changing business climate, it is imperative to have the ability to adjust to new circumstances, master new abilities, and remain significant. Creating flexibility abilities can be testing, yet it isn't unimaginable. There are a few methodologies that an individual can use to further develop their versatility abilities.

Embrace Change: One of the fundamental methodologies for creating flexibility abilities is to embrace change. Change is an unavoidable piece of life, and it is fundamental to acknowledge and embrace it. Rather than opposing change, people ought to see it as an amazing chance to learn and develop. It is fundamental to foster an uplifting perspective towards change and acknowledge it as a fundamental piece of the educational experience.

Develop a Development disposition : Which was treated in the past part. People with a development disposition accept that their capacities can be created through difficult work and commitment. They embrace provokes and view them as any open doors to learn and develop. Developing a development outlook is fundamental for creating versatility abilities. It empowers people to see change as a chance for development and learning.

Foster Flexibility: Strength is the capacity to recuperate rapidly from misfortunes, adjust to new circumstances, and quickly return more grounded. Creating versatility is fundamental for creating flexibility abilities. It empowers people to confront difficulties and defeat obstructions. Versatility can be created by zeroing in on taking care of oneself, laying out sensible objectives , and building an encouraging group of people.

Advance Constantly: Learning is fundamental for creating flexibility abilities. People ought to persistently look for new information, abilities, and encounters. They ought to be available to gain from others and attempt new things. Learning can be formal or casual, and it can take many structures, like going to studios, understanding books, or taking web-based courses.

Practice Adaptability: Adaptability is the capacity to adjust to new circumstances and evolving conditions. Rehearsing adaptability is fundamental for creating versatility abilities. It empowers people to change their arrangements and procedures on a case by case basis to accomplish their objectives. People can rehearse adaptability by being available to input, attempting new methodologies, and being willing to take a different path necessary if .

Creating versatility abilities is fundamental for flourishing in the speedy, complex, and uncertain corporate world. It expects people to embrace change, develop a development outlook, foster versatility, advance ceaselessly, and practice adaptability. By taking on these techniques, people can further develop their versatility abilities and make progress in their own and proficient lives.

CONCLUSION

At the point when we discuss The R Variable, we discuss how you answer any occasion to obtain an improved Result. No matter what, your disposition influences your exhibition and your reaction.

Your disposition significantly affects the manner in which you lead individuals. It influences the manner in which you sell and the manner in which you serve clients. Your disposition straightforwardly affects how you convey and team up with others, how you add to the way of life of your workplace, and how you play out your day to day assignments and obligations. At last, your disposition shapes your prosperity and your satisfaction. Taking everything into account, the individual with the best disposition will win. Different things not being equivalent, the individual with the best disposition typically wins. Sadly, many individuals stick to convictions and dispositions that limit them instead of engaging in their presentation.

Actually you decide your disposition . Your disposition is one of only a handful of exceptional things in life over which you have complete control. A person can change his life by modifying his mentalities of the brain. To perform at your best, and if you need to augment your joy and satisfaction, then you should assume command over the life-molding force of your disposition. If it's not too much trouble, grasp: creating and supporting an uplifting outlook isn't simply a

handy solution inspirational method. A
trained expertise should be rehearsed and
mastered.